GAL CHINATOWN KOREATOWN LITTLE IND

NEW CHINATOWN LITTLE IND

TLE SRI LANKA LITTLE BEIRUT LIT

TLE POLAND LITTLE ITALY LITTLE A

LITTLE SENEGAL CHINATOWN KO

BLIC LITTLE ATHENS LITTLE EGYPT N

LTING POT LITTLE SRI LANKA

NDIES LITTLE POLAND LITTLE ITA

TTLE BRITAIN LITTLE SENEGAL CHI

N REPUBLIC LITTLE ATHENS LITTL

A LITTLE MELTING POT LITTL

ODESSA LITTLE WEST INDIES LITTLE

ITTLE MEXICO LITTLE BRITAIN L

OMINICAN REPUBLIC LITTLE ATHE

LATIN AMERICA A LITTLE MELT

A LITTLE ODESSA LITTLE WEST

# NEW YORK: THE BIG CITY and Its LITTLE NEIGHBORHOODS

# NEW YORK: **THE BIG CITY** and Its **LITTLE NEIGHBORHOODS**

WRITTEN AND PRODUCED BY Naomi Fertitta

PHOTOGRAPHY BY Paul Aresu

UNIVERSE

**Published by UNIVERSE PUBLISHING**
A Division of Rizzoli International Publications, Inc.
300 Park Avenue South
New York, NY 10010
www.rizzoliusa.com

The NYC & Company Foundation is a 501(c)(3)
charitable and educational organization whose
mission is to support tourism to New York City
by promoting the arts and cultural organizations
that make visiting New York City a special and
exciting experience. Since its inception in 1999,
the Foundation has focused on educating
domestic and international audiences about the
vibrant and diverse cultural community throughout New York City.

All photographs © 2009 Paul Aresu

Written and produced by: Naomi Fertitta
Photographs: Paul Aresu
Project Editor: Melissa P. Veronesi
Copy Editor: Deborah T. Zindell
Design: Emily Lessard and Willy Wong

2009  2010  2011  2012 / 10  9  8  7  6  5  4  3  2  1

Printed in China

ISBN-13: 978-0-7893-1898-5

Library of Congress Catalog Control Number:
2009901019

Publisher's Note: Neither Universe Publishing nor
the author has any interest, financial or personal, in
the locations listed in this book. No fees were paid
or services rendered in exchange for inclusion in
these pages. Please note that while every effort was
made to ensure accuracy at the time of publication,
it is always best to call ahead to confirm that the
information is still up-to-date.

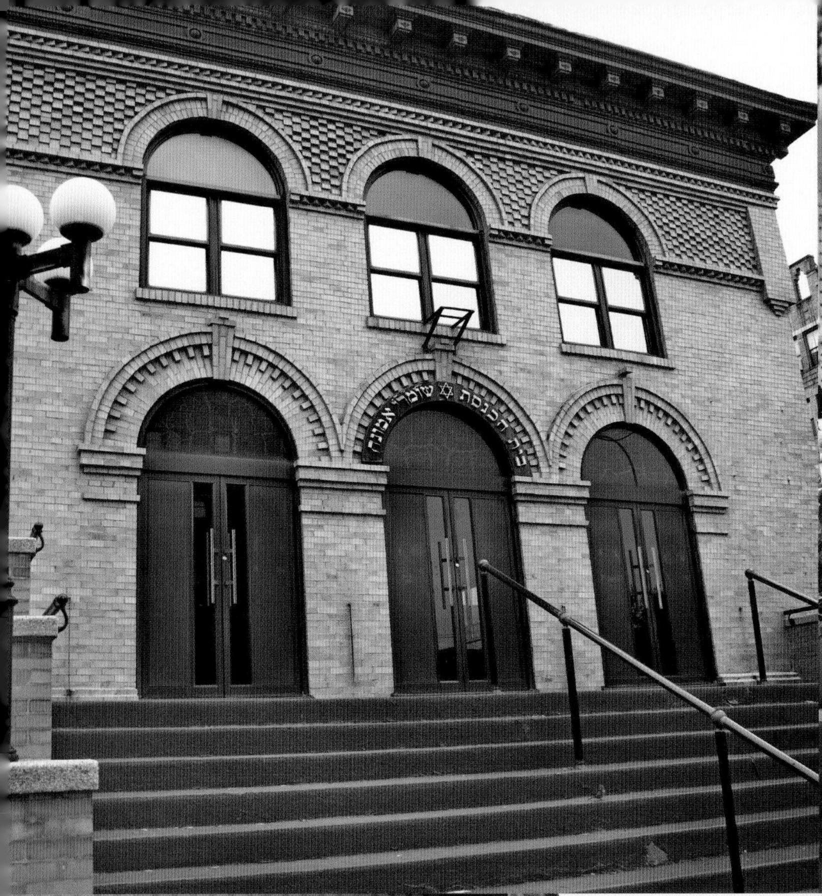

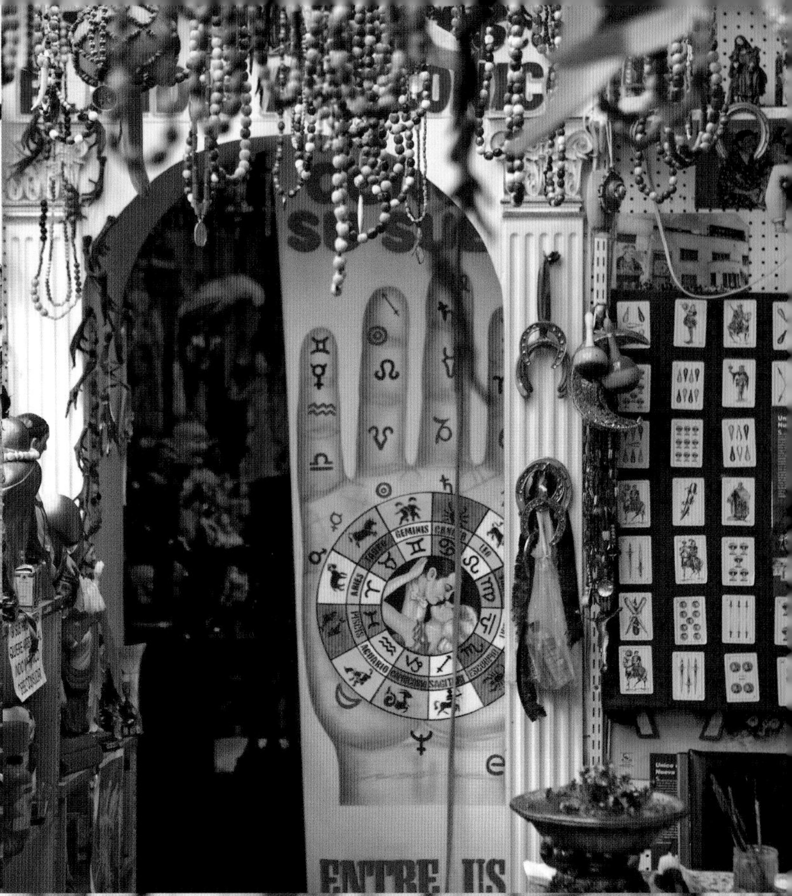

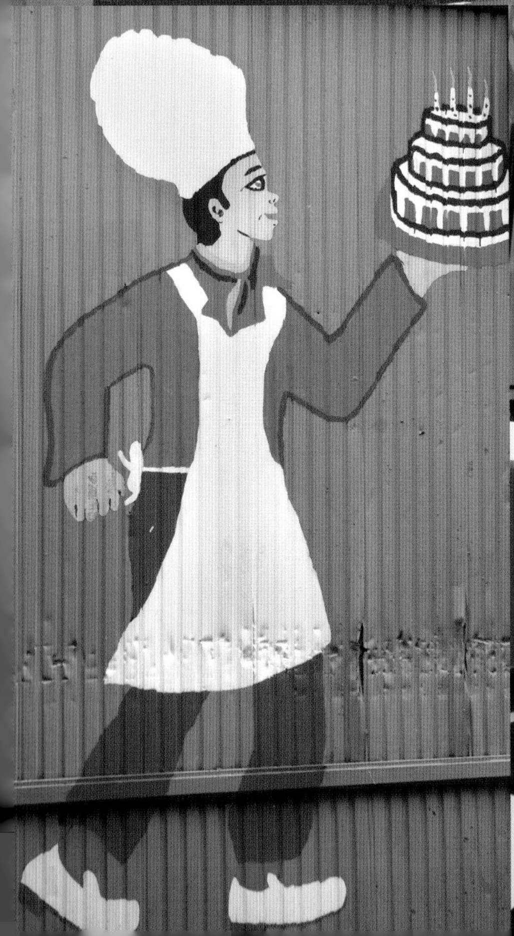

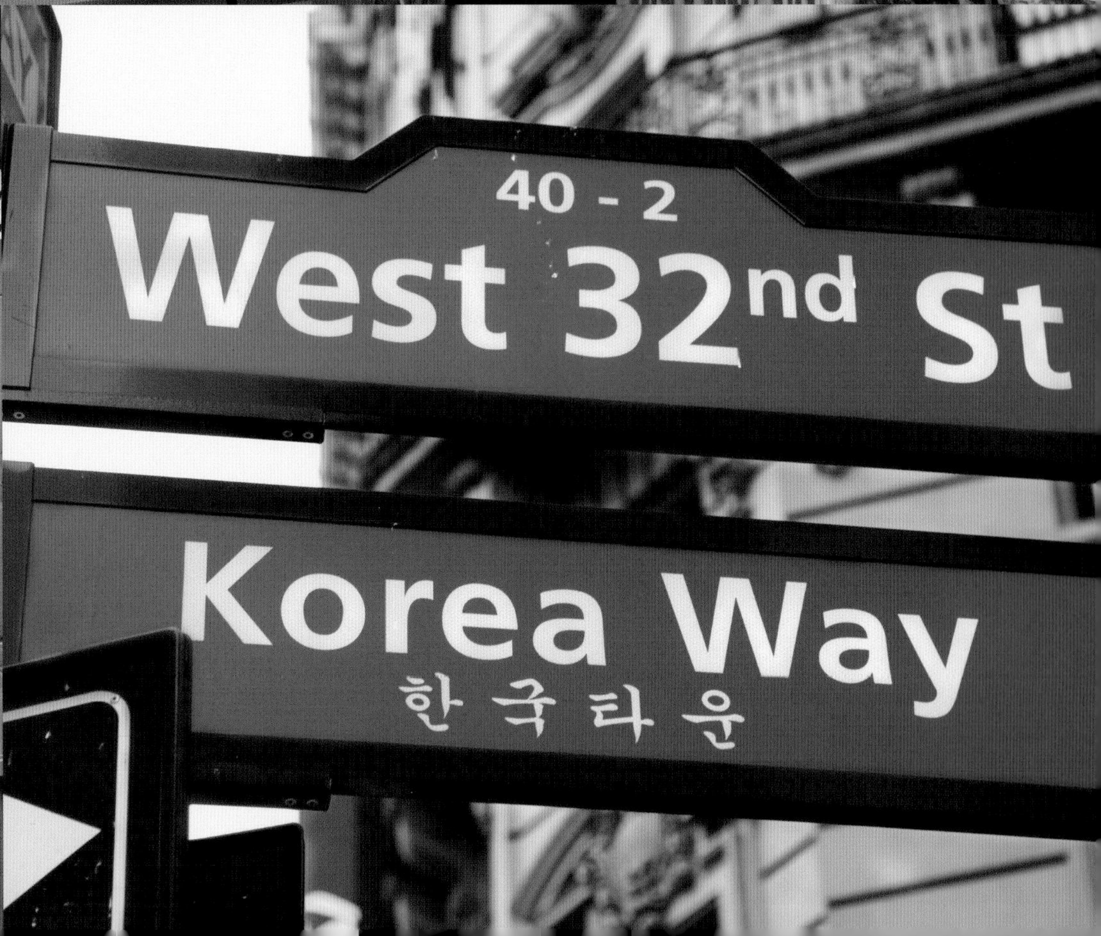
40 - 2
West 32nd St
Korea Way
한국타운

## INTRODUCTION  Naomi Fertitta

I WAS BORN IN MANHATTAN, BUT I GREW UP IN QUEENS. Ever since childhood my goal had been to move back to the borough where I was born. To my young mind, Manhattan was the embodiment of sophistication and Queens was just a provincial stop on my way to an exciting future.

Manhattan, or "The City" as we called it, was the city of my dreams. Its unimaginable glamour, sublime intensity, and absurd energy filled me with the promise of a rich and rewarding life. My city had the sophisticated sheen of uptown and the gritty hipness of downtown. It was both vast and personal, a place where I could carve out my own piece of paradise.

And that is exactly what happened. After college I moved to Manhattan and found work, love, and the infinite joys of family life. Wrapped up in this cozy cocoon, I failed to notice the city beyond the confines of my own life.

Back then, when I ventured out of Manhattan, the other boroughs were simply places I drove through to get somewhere else. But one day I realized that this city I proclaimed to love was a stranger to me. And so, really on a whim, I decided to learn about the history of different neighborhoods and explore New York City in all its infinite variety.

But first there was research to do. New York City has been called a "melting pot," and it certainly lives up to its reputation. It is a city of 26,403 people per square mile. They speak approximately 170 languages, comprise 52 ethnic groups, and 36 percent are foreign born. These

New Yorkers, old and new alike, have founded 198 ethnic newspapers and dozens of television and radio stations. But they also have created their own "little" neighborhoods across the five boroughs. The more I learned about these urban enclaves, the more I wanted to capture their spirit through words and photography.

Along with photographer Paul Aresu, I began a journey that only required a MetroCard. We soon discovered pockets around New York City that felt as exotic as Mumbai, Casablanca, Moscow, and Mexico City.

In the course of exploring 20 neighborhoods, I was humbled by the fact that not only had I been unfamiliar with the "outer" boroughs but, in fact, hardly knew these areas of Manhattan that were often only a short subway ride from my home. My great realization was that in my quest for sophistication, I had become just a provincial New Yorker who thought that the city began and ended at my front door.

But enough about me. This book is for you, the reader. My hope is that New Yorkers and visitors alike will take a journey off the beaten path of obvious destinations. In this book, you can find places to eat, shop, and visit, but perhaps as you explore and wander these streets, you'll turn a corner and discover, on your own, something unique and different. That, of course, is the beauty and adventure of New York City.

# ACKNOWLEDGMENTS

MY THANKS TO THE FOLLOWING PEOPLE:

A sincere debt of gratitude to Paul Aresu for giving of his time and talent to produce brilliant photography and for making this book such a pleasure to work on.

To everyone at Rizzoli but most especially, Jim Muschett and Melissa Veronesi for their unwavering enthusiasm, support, and kindness.

A big thank you to Willy Wong and Emily Lessard for all their patience and hard work designing a book that captures the spirit of New York City.

My thanks to the Borough Presidents' Offices of Brooklyn, The Bronx, Manhattan, Queens, and Staten Island. With special thanks to Ed Burke, Deputy Borough President of Staten Island; Terri Osborne, Director of Culture & Tourism for Queens; and Doris Quinones, Executive Director of the Bronx Tourism Council.

To Brad Fazzari for all his hard work and attention to detail and to Frederica Lauder for keeping me organized and on time with her usual good humor—I am grateful beyond words.

For inspiration and expertise I thank my husband George Fertitta, my biggest fan and best cheerleader. To my sons, Cree and Cam, who inspired me to rediscover my creative side. To my mother, and in loving memory of my father, whose parents fled oppression and crossed oceans to create a new life for themselves in New York City.

And finally to all the wonderful people living in the five boroughs of New York City whose warmth and generosity I'll always cherish.

# BROOKLYN

# BAY RIDGE'S **"Little Beirut"**

**MILES FROM GRAND CENTRAL**

11.5

**ROUTE FROM GRAND CENTRAL**

Take the 4 Subway (Downtown) to 14th Street/ Union Square. Transfer to the N Subway (Brooklyn Bound) and get off at 8th Avenue Station.

IF THE SIGHT OF AMERICAN FLAGS LINED UP LIKE SOLDIERS, side by side, on everyone's front lawn doesn't make you think of Middle America, then perhaps the small, tidy houses and quiet side streets will do the trick. Welcome to small-town America right here in Bay Ridge. But this most American of neighborhoods deep in the heart of Brooklyn has, over the past decades, taken on a distinctly new flavor.

In the recent past, this community of strong middle-class values, and an equally strong family presence, has been an enclave of mostly Irish and Italians. Today the values remain but the population now includes residents from Lebanon, Egypt, Yemen, Algeria, and Morocco. Playing off the name Bay Ridge, some locals now affectionately call their neighborhood "Little Beirut," because of its Middle Eastern flavor.

Bay Ridge, which overlooks New York Bay, was acquired by the Dutch West India Company from the Nyack Indians in 1652. The Dutch originally named it Yellow Hook after the clay-colored soil, but in 1853 the name was changed to Bay Ridge to reflect its location on a glacial ridge overlooking the bay.

Over time, this community became a summer retreat for the wealthy. Arriving by boat from Manhattan, many vacationed in the mansions built high on the bluffs of Shore Road overlooking the bay.

But times change, and during the late 19th century, Norwegian and Danish sailors, many of whom became

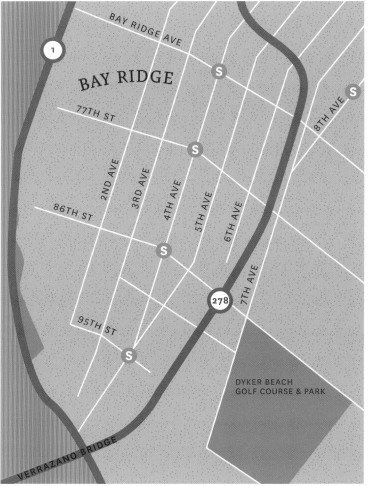

**S** = subway stop
**N** subway stop, 8th Avenue Station
**R** subway stop, Bay Ridge Avenue Station
**R** subway stop, 77th Street Station
**R** subway stop, 86th Street Station
**R** subway stop, 95th Street - Bay Ridge Station

# LITTLE BEIRUT
## NEIGHBORHOOD GUIDE

### EAT

**Areo**
*(Italian)*
8424 Third Avenue

**Ballybunion**
*(Irish bar)*
9510 Third Avenue

**Cebu**
*(Late night dining)*
8801 Third Avenue

**Omonia**
*(Greek coffee shop)*
7612-14 Third Avenue

**Tanoreen**
*(Middle Eastern)*
7704 Third Avenue

**Siwa Grill**
*(Middle Eastern)*
6917 Fifth Avenue

**Karam**
*(Middle Eastern)*
8519 Fourth Avenue

**Damascus Gate**
*(Syrian)*
7224 Fifth Avenue

**Alsalam Restaurant
and Market**
*(Middle Eastern)*
7206 Fifth Avenue

**Gino's Pizza and Pasta**
7416 Fifth Avenue

**King Falafel on Third**
*(Middle Eastern)*
7408 Third Avenue

**Les Babouche Restaurant**
*(Live band and belly
dancing on weekends)*
7803 Third Avenue

### SNACK

**Leske's Bakery**
*(Scandinavian)*
7612 Fifth Avenue

**Mejlander and
Mulganon**
*(Swedish groceries)*
7615 Fifth Avenue

**Nordic Delicacies**
*(Middle Eastern)*
6909 Third Avenue

**Najjar Pastry**
*(Middle Eastern sweets)*
7207 Fifth Avenue

### HOOKAH

**Hookah Tea Room**
9124 Fourth Avenue

### VISIT

**Historic homes on
Narrows Avenue**

**American Veterans
Memorial Pier and 9/11
Memorial**
69th Street and Shore Road

**Narrows Botanical
Garden**
Shore Road between Bay
Ridge Avenue and 72nd
Street

*And don't forget to take
in the spectacular view
of the bay and Lower
Manhattan from the
Verrazano-Narrows Bridge!*

### LITTLE BEIRUT'S
### LOCAL FLAVORS

**Shawarma**
Lebanese pita sandwich
of pit roasted beef or
duck with hummus,
tomatoes, and cucumber

**Falafel**
Chickpea patties
with tahini sauce

**Babagounough**
Mashed eggplant with spices

**Kibbe**
Minced lamb, wheat germ,
spices, and pine nuts

**Couscous**
with raisins, almonds, and
chicken or lamb

**Shish Kebabs of
Mixed Meats**

**Tagine of Chicken**
Chicken stew with
preserved lemon

carpenters and worked in the building trades, settled in Bay Ridge. Interestingly, around the turn of the 20th century, there was another group of immigrants—Christian Lebanese—who immigrated to the area.

With the extension of the subway line in 1915, it was easier to commute to this quiet, peaceful area and so Bay Ridge soon expanded with the influx of Irish and Italian immigrants. In recent years, and most likely because of the Lebanese immigrants of the early 20th century, it comes as no surprise that this oldest of Arab neighborhoods has become home to another generation of Middle Easterners. This new generation can find comfort in such places as the Salam Arabic Lutheran Church, which was formerly a Danish congregation that served the Scandinavian community of Bay Ridge since 1895.

Today there's room for everyone in Bay Ridge. One- and two- family homes retain their peaceful nature and some even have views of the majestic Verrazano-Narrows Bridge, completed in 1964 and connecting Brooklyn and Staten Island. The shops, restaurants, and bars along Third, Fourth, and Fifth Avenues still have the feel of an Irish/Italian neighborhood, with little Nordic touches here and there, but you can often find an Irish pub next door to a shop selling brightly colored hookahs and jewel-like sweets and candied fruits.

Come any day to Dyker Beach Park, and you'll see older Italian men playing bocce or fishing off the bay. On Fifth Avenue, you might also see elderly gentlemen, women, and children heading off to the Islamic Society

of Bay Ridge. Come at Christmastime for the most extraordinary display of lights decorating the neighborhood homes. Or take a stroll on a warm mid-May day and enjoy some great Italian food, buy a round of drinks at an Irish bar, listen to Arabic music, or watch the Scandinavian Day Parade with locals. 🖐

# BOROUGH PARK'S "Little Jerusalem"

**MILES FROM GRAND CENTRAL**

12.8

**ROUTE FROM GRAND CENTRAL**

Take the 7 Subway (Westbound) to 5th Avenue Station. Transfer to the D Subway (Brooklyn Bound) and get off at 50th Street Station.

ONCE A HIGHLY DIVERSE NEIGHBORHOOD, Borough (commonly spelled Boro) Park is now the heart of Orthodox Judaism in the City of New York. Walk down these streets on any weekday morning, and you'll witness bearded men dressed in black hats, with long black suits over white shirts, and prayer shawls peeking out from beneath their jackets as they rush to prayers and work. The women are also solemnly attired, dressed in black with their heads covered by a hat or wig as a sign of piety, modesty, and tradition. The sea of black and white dress, paired with the humble 1930s-style buildings, makes you feel as though you're part of a historic photograph. But don't let the somber dress fool you; Boro Park is a bustling community brimming with life.

Here in "Little Jerusalem," the largest Jewish community outside Israel, Hasidic Jews have maintained their faith, traditions, and customs for almost 80 years.

The Hasidic sect was founded in Poland around the same time the Dutch were settling in Brooklyn. The Dutch farmed the rich soil of Boro Park, or New Utrecht, as it was called then. The verdant landscape of lush farmlands, horticultural nurseries, and windmills prevailed.

Development of New Utrecht began in earnest toward the end of the 19th century. Electus B. Litchfield, a developer, built numerous homes, and the area was grandly renamed Blythebourne. For a time, this predominately Protestant neighborhood managed to maintain its rural character. But at the turn of the century, the area grew and by 1902, a Catholic church, St. Catherine of Alexander, was erected. Blythebourne's first synagogue was established two years later. By 1910, Russian Jews from the lower East Side of Manhattan were moving to Blythebourne. As transportation and housing became more accessible, the area (now incorporated into Boro Park) continued to attract more Jewish residents from other parts of New York.

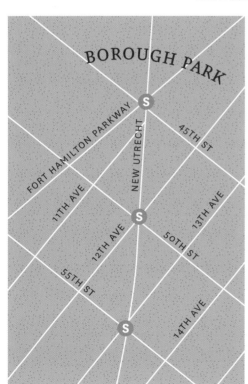

**S** = subway stop
**D, M** subway stop, Fort Hamilton Parkway Station
**D, M** subway stop, 50th Street Station
**D, M** subway stop, 55th Street Station

# LITTLE JERUSALEM
## NEIGHBORHOOD GUIDE

## EAT

**Shem Tov Manor**
*(Deli)*
5320 New Utrecht Avenue

**China Glatt**
*(Chinese)*
4413 13th Avenue

**Crown Deli**
4909 13th Avenue

**Amnon Kosher Pizza**
4814 13th Avenue

**Glatt a la carte**
*(Steakhouse)*
5123 18th Avenue

**Spoons**
*(American)*
5001 13th Avenue

## SNACK

**Strauss Bakery**
5115 13th Avenue

**Weiss Homemade
Kosher Bakery**
5011 13th Avenue

**Oh Nuts**
*(Dried fruits and nuts)*
4923 13th Avenue

**The Candyman**
4702 13th Avenue

**Schick's Bakery**
4710 16th Avenue

**Meisner Take Home
Food**
5410 New Utrecht Avenue

**Podrigal's Bakery**
1272 56th Street

**Shlomie's Bakery**
5017 New Utrecht Avenue
(between 50th and 51st
Streets)

**Yossi's Bakery & Sweet
House**
4406 14th Avenue

**Shmura Matzoh Bakery**
*(Best matzoh)*
36th Street and 13th Avenue

## SHOP

**Gal Paz**
*(Jewish music)*
4616 13th Avenue

**Mostly Music**
*(Jewish music)*
4815 13th Avenue

**Silver Town**
*(Sterling silver objects)*
4615 13th Avenue

**Eichlers Bookstore**
*(Books & religious objects)*
5004 13th Avenue

## VISIT

**Museum of the
Living Torah**
*(Call for an appointment)*
1601 41st Street
718-686-8174

**Congregation
Minyan Mar**
5401 16th Avenue

**Congregation Shomrei
Shabbos**
1280 53rd Street

---

### LITTLE JERUSALEM'S
### LOCAL FLAVORS

*This neighborhood is
famous for its baked goods.
Be sure to try:*

**Challah**
Braided bread made for the
Sabbath and Jewish holidays

**Mandelbrot**
Almond cookies

**Rugelach**
Rolled pastry filled with nuts,
raisins, or chocolate

**Hamantaschen**
A three-cornered pastry
stuffed with your choice
of poppy seeds, nuts,
prunes, or apricots for the
holiday of Purim

LITTLE JERUSALEM

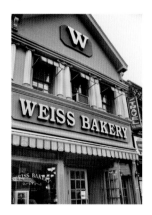

By 1930, Boro Park's community was primarily Jewish, Irish, and Italian. But it was the Jewish population that increased most quickly, partially owing to circumstances in Eastern Europe. Near the end of the 1930s, Hasidic Jews from Poland settled here to escape persecution in their homeland; a second significant influx of Hasidic Jews arrived in Boro Park in 1956, as a result of the Hungarian uprising.

Boro Park today is the same warm, welcoming community it was in the 1930s. From Sunday through Friday afternoon, the streets are filled with shoppers chattering away in Yiddish, Hebrew, Russian, and English; the store signs also reflect this mix of languages. On 13th Avenue, affectionately nicknamed the "Avenue of Values," you can find kosher bakeries filled with decadent desserts, kosher candy shops featuring a rainbow of goodies from all over the world, religious book stores, exuberant Jewish music stores, shops displaying a treasure trove of sterling silver vases, menorahs, and other religious objects, and others selling any Jewish novelty item and collectible imaginable. But remember, religion informs the rhythm of the streets; from sundown on Friday until Saturday evening, everything closes down for the Sabbath, and that includes the myriad of restaurants that line the avenues. From kosher Chinese food, pizza, deli items, fast food, and grand steakhouses, Boro Park has it all—

but it's best, of course, to visit these favorite spots during the week.

Everywhere in Boro Park is the opportunity to experience this unique community's customs and faith. Visit Congregation Shomrei Shabbos, the busiest synagogue in the world. Men stream in and out of the synagogue from 9:00 a.m. to 2:15 a.m. for more than 150 minyans (prayers) a day. There are hundreds of other synagogues that also meet the needs of the great variety of Hasidic sects, such as Bobov, Belz, Ger, Satmar, as well as the community's non-Hasidic Orthodox Jews.

And be sure to visit the world's only museum devoted to biblical archaeology, The Living Torah Museum, a small, humble affair filled with a vast array of fascinating ancient artifacts. But what's unique about this museum is that it is a "hands on" museum that permits its visitors to hold the ancient objects and touch the past. This charming museum may well be seen as a metaphor for the entire neighborhood. Boro Park is a place not only to experience a thriving, growing community, but also a place where you can touch the past. ⁑

# BRIGHTON BEACH'S "Little Odessa"

**ROUTE FROM GRAND CENTRAL**

Take the 7 Subway (Westbound) to 5th Avenue Station. Transfer to the B Subway (Brooklyn Bound) and get off at Brighton Beach Station.

IF YOU WANT TO FEEL LIKE YOU ARE TRAVELING TO ANOTHER COUNTRY, Brighton Beach is just a short subway ride away. Under the arches of the elevated train, between Manhattan Beach and Coney Island, lives a secret showplace, a cosmopolitan enclave full of displaced Russian Jews replicating a dream of forgotten Russia.

Brighton Beach, affectionately called "Little Odessa" after the city in the Ukraine, where much of its population traces its roots, exudes an Old World charm. Brighton Beach Avenue—a busy and vibrant boulevard—is home to Russian food emporiums, bookstores, newsstands, nightclubs, restaurants, and cafés. A few blocks over, there's a wide boardwalk that hugs a broad beach.

It's the sea air that, well over a century ago, inspired wealthy businessmen to create a seaside destination for the upper class. Wanting to emulate the sophisticated town of Brighton in the south of England, developers built the Hotel Brighton on Coney Island Avenue in 1869. Nine years later, the Brighton Beach Bathing Pavilion and Ocean Pier opened. This establishment offered not only proximity to the beach, but also entertainment. They featured the Lilliputian Opera Company as well as popular music and vaudeville. And for those who were of a betting nature, there was horse racing. The track opened in 1879 but closed in 1910 due to anti-betting laws. This closing led to the demise of most of Brighton Beach's greatest showplaces. The area still had its boardwalk and sea breezes, but its moments of grandeur had passed and the wealthy residents moved on.

The change in circumstances in Brighton Beach allowed for Eastern European Jews from the Lower Eastside and Brownsville, who were looking to escape tumbled-down tenements, to

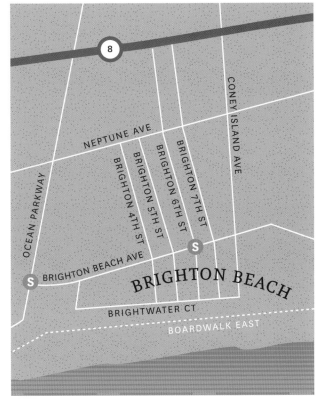

S = subway stop
**Q** subway stop, Ocean Parkway Station
**B, Q** subway stop, Brighton Beach Station

# LITTLE ODESSA
## NEIGHBORHOOD GUIDE

## EAT

**Café Arbat**
306 Brighton Beach Avenue

**Moscow Café**
3152 Brighton 6th Street

**Gina's Café**
409 Brighton Beach Avenue

**Rasputin Supper Club**
2670 Coney Island Avenue

**Tatiana Restaurant**
3152 Brighton 6th Street

**The National**
273 Brighton Beach Avenue

## EAT: ON THE BOARDWALK

**Winter Garden Restaurant**
3152 Brighton 6th Street

**Odessa Restaurant**
1113 Brighton Beach Avenue

## SHOP

**M & I International Foods**
249 Brighton Beach Avenue

**Vintage Food Corp.**
287 Brighton Beach Avenue

**St. Petersburg Bookstore**
230 Brighton Beach Avenue

**Gastronome Odessa Incorporated**
1117 Brighton Beach Avenue

## VISIT

**The Boardwalk**
*Watch old men play chess or just take in the ocean breeze.*

### LITTLE ODESSA'S LOCAL FLAVORS

**Borscht**
Beet soup with sour cream

**Eggplant with Walnuts**

**Pelmeni**
Dumplings filled with meat, cheese, or potatoes

**Blini with Caviar**

**Kupaty**
Georgian sausage

**Solyanka**
Shredded lamb in coriander sauce

**Chakapuli**
Braised veal with spinach

move to the area. With them, they brought a rich cultural heritage. Soon the music hall became a Yiddish theater, and fancy restaurants offered Russian Jewish fare. There were knishes, smoked fish, bagels, bialys, and other basic Russian food. In place of the racetrack, there were now handball tournaments, water shows, card games, and knish-eating contests.

By the 1920s, Brighton Beach had evolved from a summer playground to a year-round neighborhood of apartments and houses from Coney Island Avenue to Ocean Parkway. In the 1930s into the 1940s, Jewish immigrants, who were escaping the atrocities of the Nazis, settled here as well as in other New York neighborhoods. By the 1950s, the residents were mostly second-generation Americans as well as Holocaust survivors.

The 1960s and 1970s saw this once vibrant neighborhood fall into a period of steep decline. The steadily growing elderly population combined with a rising crime rate held little promise for Brighton Beach. But by the 1980s and 1990s, Jewish immigrants from the former Soviet Union moved here and revitalized this community.

Today, the boulevard that runs under the train tracks is overflowing with Russian stores, restaurants, and cafés, many with store signs written in Cyrillic. If you long for Russian food, this is paradise. These immaculate stores offer smoked meats and an unbelievable array of smoked fish, caviar, cheese, and Russian black bread. The quantities of food are dizzying. The restaurants offer pirogues, Chicken Kiev, blini caviar, borscht, kebabs, and meat-filled dumplings.

If you come at night you must experience a Russian nightclub. From the Vegas-style floorshows and the Russian techno music, you can experience the Russian culture first-hand. Make sure to taste some of the Russian vodka (usually on every table in the clubs), and you can feel as if you've been transported to another place and another time. ≋

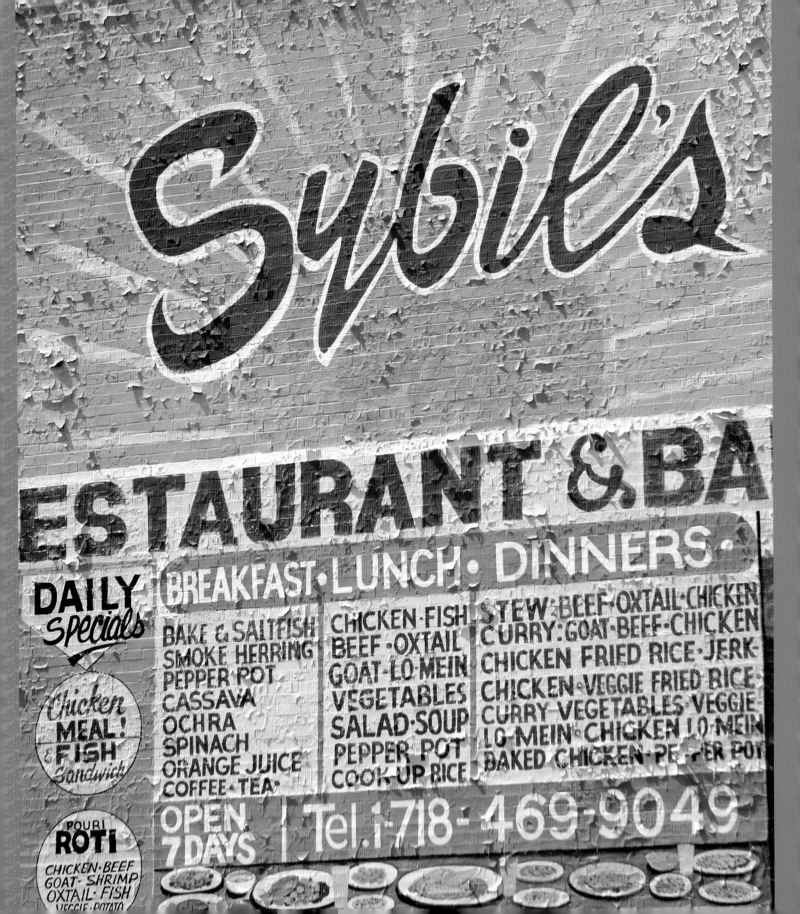

# FLATBUSH'S "Little West Indies"

**MILES FROM GRAND CENTRAL**

10.2

**ROUTE FROM GRAND CENTRAL**

Take the 5 Subway (Downtown) to 14th Street/Union Square. Transfer to the Q Subway (Brooklyn Bound) and get off at Beverley Road Station

THE NAME FLATBUSH MAY NOT EXACTLY INSPIRE VISIONS of the Caribbean for most people, but the residents of Brooklyn know better. Here in this working-class neighborhood you'll find immigrants from Jamaica, Trinidad, Barbados, Guyana, Tobago, Haiti, and Saint Vincent, and they've made this pocket of Brooklyn all their own.

Though some of today's Web bloggers, in an effort to gentrify the area, have given Flatbush the new nickname NoProPaSo (North of Prospect Park South), a more well-known nickname, Little West Indies, reflects its essence and its residents, rather than merely its geography.

There was a time when Flatbush was the town of Midwout, a wooded tract of land that was part of the Dutch colony of Nieuw Nederland established in 1651. Locals also referred to the area as Vladbos (wooded land), which, when anglicized upon its surrender to the English, became Flatbush. Despite losing to the British, however, a number of Dutch families remained in the area continuing to farm and run businesses. Even as late as the 1860s and 1870s, Flatbush's landscape was still dotted with windmills.

In 1894, Flatbush was incorporated into Brooklyn. The area became a rural, suburban enclave that boasted large Victorian houses surrounded by cool shade trees. But this period in Flatbush's history was short-lived. When the Coney Island Railroad came along, so did real estate developers. Now, with easy access to businesses in Manhattan, the developers saw an opportunity for large-scale housing for an emerging middle class. By the 1920s, there was a new population of residents on Ocean Avenue: Jews, Italians,

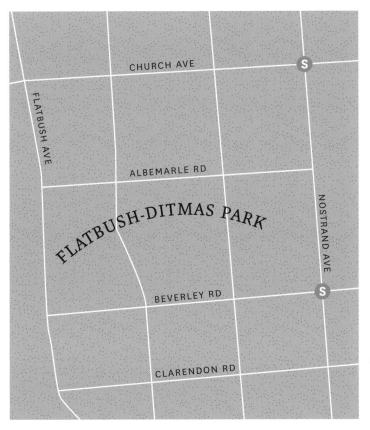

**S** = subway stop
2, 5 subway stop, Beverley Road Station
2, 5 subway stop, Church Avenue Station

and African Americans who had left their overcrowded neighborhoods.

This new group left its stamp on Flatbush's character, and this now bustling neighborhood became known for its grand movie palaces and Ebbets Field, the home of the Brooklyn Dodgers before they went west. (Because neighborhood boundaries have changed, Ebbets Field would today be in Crown Heights.) But as with many other neighborhoods in New York City, the younger generation moved out, leaving room for a new wave. By the 1980s, Flatbush had taken on a distinctly Caribbean flavor.

This neighborhood truly is a taste of the islands. Go into any market, and you'll find the store shelves stocked with every conceivable brand of hot sauce, rubs for jerk chicken, and drinks like sorrel and ginger beer. Go to a local restaurant and eat Trinidadian rotis (think Caribbean burrito) or Barbadian cou-cou with flying fish, or try a bakery that offers callal-loo rolls and bread pudding.

Besides the food markets, the shops and street vendors also give off an unmistakable Caribbean-centric vibe. Here you'll find no shortage of Jamaican music shops, dread-locked vendors selling jewelry, T-shirts, hats, and even bikinis in the colors of the different island flags. Flatbush pulses with the energy and joy of its people. After a day in Flatbush, wandering down Church Street or Flatbush Avenue surrounded by crowds of people shopping, eating, or just hanging out, you just might begin to sway with the rhythms of the Caribbean and feel a soft ocean breeze right here in Brooklyn. ₽⁘

**100% PURE COCONUT WATER**
FROM JAMAICA
AVAILABLE IN STORES
"COCONUT WATER, GOOD FE YU DAWTA"
NO PRESERVATIVES
ORDER CALL: 347-234-0445

FRIED SHARK Sold HERE #4.00 Per Serving

**HOT DRINKS**
• TEA • COFFEE • MILK • SOUP
• MILO • OVALTINE
• HOT CHOCOLATE
**COLD DRINKS**
• SORREL • MAUBY
• SOURSOP • SEA MOSS
• PEANUT PUNCH • CARROT JUICE
• ORANGE JUICE
SODAS / West Indian SODAS

# LITTLE WEST INDIES
## NEIGHBORHOOD GUIDE

### EAT

**Badoo's International Restaurant**
5422 Church Avenue

**Choices Caribbean Restaurant**
1640 Nostrand Avenue

**Donna's Jerk Chicken**
3125 Church Avenue

**Guyana Roti House**
3021 Church Avenue

**Jerk City**
3402 Church Avenue

**Jimbo Jean Jamaican Restaurant**
2223 Church Avenue

**Mike's Island Grill Restaurant**
2223 Tilden Avenue

### SNACK

**Angel's Flake Patties**
2114 Nostrand Avenue

**Golden Krust Bakery**
931 Flatbush Avenue

**Hammond's Bakery and Jerk Center**
1033 Nostrand Avenue

**Sybil's Bakery & Restaurant**
2110 Church Avenue

**Nio's Trinidad Roti and Bakery**
2702 Church Street

**Tamarind Tree**
1463 Flatbush Avenue

### SHOP

*Shop the street vendors and...*

**Flatbush Caton Market**
*Market with 45 vendors that houses everything from Caribbean themed items to fashion and a farmers market*
794-814 Flatbush Avenue

### VISIT

**Flatbush Dutch Reformed Church**
*(Founded by Peter Stuyvesant in 1654)*
890 Flatbush Avenue

**Salem Missionary Baptist Church**
East 21st Street and Albemarle Road

**Flatbush Historic District**
East 21st Street and Church Avenue

**Flatbush Town Hall**
35 Snyder Avenue

**Johannes Van Nuys House**
1128 East 34th Street between Avenue J and Flatbush Avenue

**JAMERIFRICAN**
*We Sell All Kinds of*
TAPES · HANDBAGS · T-SHIRTS
CAPS · PERFUMES · BATTERIES

### LITTLE WEST INDIES' LOCAL FLAVORS

**Callaloo Soup**

**Ackee and Codfish**
with roasted breadfruit

**Jerk Chicken and Pork**

**Curried Goat**
with rice and peas

**Bulla Cake**

**Spice Bun**
with fruit

**Jamaican Patties**

**Sorrel or Mango Juice**

**Ginger Beer**

# GREENPOINT'S "Little Poland"

**MILES FROM GRAND CENTRAL**

3.7

**ROUTE FROM GRAND CENTRAL**

Take the 7 Subway (Queensbound) to Court House Square. Transfer to the G Subway (Brooklyn Bound) and get off at Nassau Avenue Station.

THERE'S AN UNMISTAKABLE EASTERN EUROPEAN VIBE here in Greenpoint, a lively community that borders the East River in northernmost Brooklyn. And with good reason, because this working-class neighborhood is home to the second largest Polish community in America, after Chicago. The area is known as "Little Poland," where many storefronts proclaim "Mowlmy po Polsko" (We speak Polish) and the sweet scents of periogi and kielbasa hang in the air. But here in Greenpoint, there are also other signs—signs of change. "Polish" Greenpoint is evolving into "Hipster" Greenpoint. So, when you come and visit here, be prepared to plant your feet into very different worlds.

Like many areas in the five boroughs, the Dutch once claimed this area as its own. In 1638, a small group settled here, drawn to this lovely peninsula of rivers, creeks, and marshes; in fact, Greenpoint took its name from this grassy promontory that jutted into the river. It's hard to imagine that the hustle and bustle of today's Greenpoint was inhabited by just five families for almost 200 years. This rich land was cultivated, creating lush farmlands and orchards, but it was an area lacking a store, a church, or even a school.

This is how it remained until the construction of the first public highway in 1838. Greenpoint transformed from private farms and homes into a small town. Because of its proximity to waterways, it became a center for the shipbuilding industry and was instrumental in building the first ironclad warship, the USS Monitor for use during the Civil War.

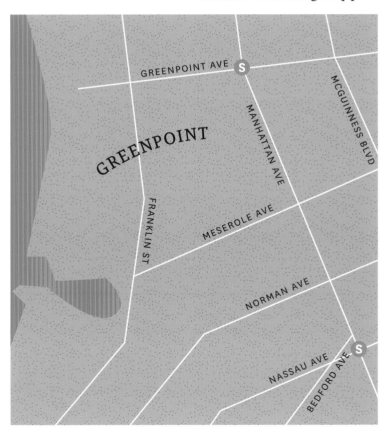

**S** = subway stop
**G** subway stop, Greenpoint Avenue Station
**G** subway stop, Nassau Avenue Station

# LITTLE POLAND
## NEIGHBORHOOD GUIDE

## EAT

**Pyza**
118 Nassau Avenue

**Jagienka Restaurant**
152 Driggs Avenue

**Lomzynianka**
646 Manhattan Avenue

**Old Poland**
192 Nassau Avenue

**Polska Restauracja**
136 Greenpoint Avenue

**Krolewskie Jadlo
(King's Feast)**
694 Manhattan Avenue

✔ **Peter Pan Donut and
Pastry Shop**
*(Best Donuts)*
727 Manhattan Avenue

## EAT: PORK

**Steve's Meat Market**
104 Nassau Avenue

✔ **Sirkorski Meat Market**
603 Manhattan Avenue

**Polam International
Meat Market**
952 Manhattan Avenue

✔ **West Nassau Meat
Market**
915 Manhattan Avenue

## SHOP: DISCOUNT

**Vortex Thrift Shop**
1084 Manhattan Avenue

**Dee & Dee**
777 Manhattan Avenue

**Mary's Discount Store**
664 Manhattan Avenue

**Fashion Plaza**
958 Manhattan Avenue

## SHOP: HIP & MODERN

**Alter**
*(Men's & women's fashions)*
109 Franklin Street

**Dalaga**
*(Men's & women's fashions)*
150 Franklin Street

**Hayden-Harnett**
*(Leather goods)*
211 Franklin Street

**Permanent Records**
*(New and used CDs, LPs,
and 45s)*
181 Franklin Street

## NIGHTLIFE/BARS

**Dami's**
931 Manhattan Avenue

**Diamond Bar**
43 Franklin Street

**Black Rabbit**
91 Greenpoint Avenue

**Studio B**
259 Banker Street

## VISIT

**McCarren Park**
*30-acre park between
Bedford and Driggs Avenues*

**Greenpoint Historic
District**
*Beautiful architecture
located on Kent, Calyer,
Noble, and Franklin Streets,
Clifford Place, Lorimer Street,
and Manhattan Avenue*

**Shelter Pavilion and
Monument to the
U.S.S. Monitor and U.S.S.
Merrimack**
Monsignor McGolrick Park

### LITTLE POLAND'S LOCAL FLAVORS

**Boczek ze Silwka**
Bacon stuffed prunes

**Smalec**
Fried onion and lard served
with bread and
pickled cucumber

**Sztuka Mięsa w
Sosie Chrzanowym**
Boiled beef in
horseradish sauce

**Kielbasa**
Polish sausage

**Zeberka w Miodzie**
Spare ribs with honey

**Bigos**
Hunter Stew with various
meats and sauerkraut

**Cheese, Meat, and
Potato Pierogis**

Other industries developed here as well, including pottery, glassmaking, printing, and refineries. The abundance of work lured new immigrants to Greenpoint, and by the end of the nineteenth century Irish, Russian, Italians, and Poles had settled here.

The second wave of Polish immigrants came during the 1930s and 1940s. First came Polish arrivals escaping Hitler's army, and then in the 1940s, Poles came fleeing Stalin's tyranny. Many of these immigrants replicated the flavor of the old country in their new surroundings as they tried to assimilate while preserving their own identity. A third wave of immigration occurred after the fall of the Soviet Union in the late 1980s.

From the beginning, religion and the church played a central role in the life of these new immigrants. Uncomfortable in non-Polish churches, the residents of Greenpoint set about, at great financial sacrifice, to establish Polish churches throughout their community.

Many of these churches are in the designated historic district of Greenpoint, a five-block area from Calyer Street to Kent Street and from

Manhattan Avenue to Humboldt Street. Saint Stanislaus Kostka Roman Catholic Church on Humboldt boasts the largest congregation in Brooklyn and is one of the treasures of this charming historic area. Other churches within this district include The Episcopal Church of the Ascension on Kent Street and the Russian Orthodox Cathedral of the Transfiguration of Our Lord on North 12th Street. It is not without a certain irony that this area, which didn't have a church for 200 years, is now renowned for its many beautiful churches.

But that's not all you'll find in the historic district. The Astral Apartments and the Eberhard-Faber Pencil Factory on Franklin Street are fine examples of architecture. Remember too, that this area is mostly residential with charming townhouses and homes that make you feel as if you stepped into the 19th century.

While you're in Greenpoint, visit McCarren Park, the largest in the area situated on 35 acres. Here the residents play soccer, volleyball, softball, and other recreational sports. In recent years, every June, the locals hold the Renegade Craft Fair selling everything from jewelry to clothing and paper goods as well as art.

Don't forget about the food in Greenpoint. On Manhattan Avenue, the main shopping area which offers great views of Manhattan, are butcher shops that are a carnivore's dream. Pork is king, and you'll find kielbasa, air-dried sausage, and fresh sausage hanging from the ceiling. The flavors are both sweet and salty and have a rich and addictive quality. But there's not just sausage; Greenpoint has an amazing selection of smoked pork loin, fresh bacon, rustic pâtés, and stews. If you need some side dishes, pick up fresh sauerkraut, pickles, and Polish rye bread.

Check out the family-run restaurants that are inexpensive and plentiful. On the bilingual menus you'll find stuffed cabbage, sauerkraut and beef, white borscht, and the ever-present kielbasa sausage. If you have room for dessert, try one of the old-fashioned shops where young Polish girls in candy-colored costumes serve donuts.

While Greenpoint still retains some of its Old World flavor there's a fast-growing community of young, hip, creative types making its home here. Instead of just going to the Polish National Home for Entertainment, you can also go to bars and clubs where indie bands play frequently. Or go on a bar crawl and try Brooklyn's hand-crafted beers. The great thing about Greenpoint is you can choose which world you want to be in, or, better yet, come here and experience all sides of this historic, vibrant, and constantly evolving Brooklyn community. ⚓

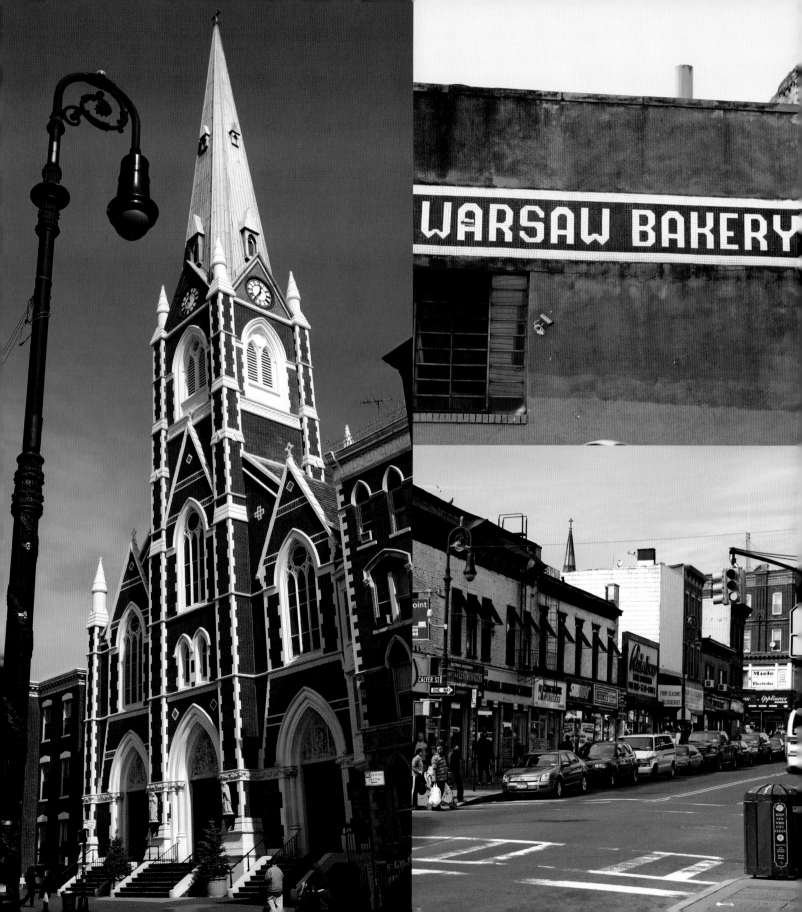

WOODLAWN

BELMONT

# BRONX

# BELMONT'S "Little Italy" & "Little Albania"

**MILES FROM GRAND CENTRAL**

12

**ROUTE FROM GRAND CENTRAL**

Take the 4 Subway (Uptown) and get off at Fordham Road Station.

ANYONE LOOKING FOR A GOOD TIME WITH THE LOCALS needs only take a trip to Arthur Avenue in the Belmont section of the Bronx. Once there, you might just get the idea that you're in a Martin Scorsese movie. Nowhere else will you find a more colorful cast of characters than those living in this part of New York City. The people who live here are tough, warm, and welcoming. Belmont's convivial atmosphere came out of a long-established Italian neighborhood that now is also home to a growing Albanian population. These East Europeans, like many generations of their countrymen that preceded them to the five boroughs, are gradually putting their stamp on this close-knit community.

Belmont does boast a lively immigrant population, but its history is a bit different from that of other similar neighborhoods in that the area originally started out as a grand estate. Land that is now The New York Botanical Garden to the northeast and the Bronx Zoo to the east and stretches all the way to St. Barnabas Hospital to the south was once the estate of the Lorillard family, who made its fortune in tobacco and was involved in thoroughbred horse racing (Pierre Lorillard's horse "Saxon" won the Belmont Stakes in 1876). Though the family sold its home and property in 1870, one of the more visible remnants of its presence remains—Arthur Avenue is named after President Chester A. Arthur, whom the Lorillard family greatly admired.

But Arthur Avenue took on a decidedly different flavor at the turn of the 20th century. The Lorillard's grand home and verdant fields were transformed into housing for a new wave of Sicilian immigrants. Always a close-knit community, these

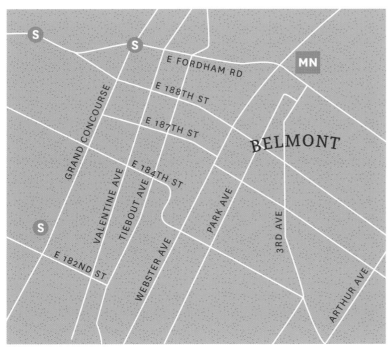

**S** = subway stop   **MN** = Metro-North stop

**4** subway stop, Fordham Road Station at Jerome Ave

**B, D** subway stop, Fordham Road Station at Grand Concourse

**B, D** subway stop, 182nd Street Station

**Metro-North** train stop, Fordham Station

# LITTLE ITALY & LITTLE ALBANIA
## NEIGHBORHOOD GUIDE

### EAT

**Ann & Tony's**
2407 Arthur Avenue

✔ **Emilia's**
2331 Arthur Avenue

**Full Moon Pizzeria**
600 East 187th Street

**Dominick's**
2335 Arthur Avenue

**Gurra Café**
*(Albanian)*
2325 Arthur Avenue

**Pasquale Rigoletto**
2311 Arthur Avenue

### SNACK

**Artuso Pastry**
670 East 187th Street

**Café Santa**
660 East 187th Street

**Mike's Deli at the Arthur Avenue Retail Market**
2344 Arthur Avenue

### SHOP

**Addeo Bakery**
2372 Hughes Avenue

**Borgatti's Ravioli and Egg Noodles**
632 East 187th Street

**Madonia Brothers Bakery**
2348 Arthur Avenue

✔ **Teitel Brothers**
2372 Arthur Avenue

✔ **Calandra Cheese**
2314 Arthur Avenue

**Kosova European Meat and Grocery**
2326 Arthur Avenue

**Arthur Avenue Retail Market**
2344 Arthur Avenue
*Here you'll find food stalls with fresh produce, pasta, pizza, sausage, cured meats, baked goods, and homemade cigars.*

### VISIT

**The Bronx Zoo**
183rd Street and Southern Boulevard

✔ **The New York Botanical Garden**
Bronx River Parkway at East Fordham Road

**Enrico Fermi Cultural Center at the Belmont New York Public Library**
610 East 186th Street

**Our Lady of Mount Carmel Church**
627 East 187th Street

### LITTLE ITALY'S & LITTLE ALBANIA'S LOCAL FLAVORS

*The Italian food here is endless and you'll find everything from homemade cheese and pastas to tiramisu and tartufo. But also try the Albanian specialties:*

**Pasulj**
Serbian bean soup

**Qebapa**
Beef and lamb meatballs

**Qofte**
Minced beef with onion, parsley, and mint

**Pleskavice**
An Albanian shish-kebab

*1/2/2010*

new residents quickly established their old-world traditions in this corner of the Bronx. They brought with them their faith, the reverence for family, continuity, and stability, and their work ethic. Generations

later these traditions still exist, giving Belmont the feel of a small town where almost everyone seems to know one another. As in the past, Our Lady of Mount Carmel Church is still the spiritual heart of Belmont, and many of the surrounding businesses have been passed down from generation to generation.

Of course there's another tradition that's paramount to this neighborhood—the love of great food. Where peddlers and pushcarts once plied their wares, today you can find an old fashioned indoor food market housing everything from hand-crafted cigars to homemade mozzarella.

Belmont, and more specifically Arthur Avenue, has always been a mecca for tourists. After all, within this small area you can find more than 50 restaurants and cafés plus markets and delis. This is a food buyer's paradise. On Saturdays, the sidewalks are crammed with locals and not-so-locals rushing in and out of the green markets buying from the colorful mosaic displays of fruits and vegetables, or you can see the butchers showing off their vast array of meats and plump sausages, or visit the cheese shops, fish markets, wine merchants, or bakeries that sell fresh bread, cannolis, biscotti, and every form of pasta imaginable.

But if you take a deep breath and look a little closer, you can also see the residents savoring an espresso outside their social club or enjoying a meal at an outdoor café; men sitting on lawn chairs on the sidewalk smoking cigars and listening to Frank Sinatra; generations of families loudly laughing, talking, and enjoying the neighborhood that they'll never forget. Every one of them will likely tell you that there's no other place to be but here. ♧

# WOODLAWN'S "Little Ireland"

**MILES FROM
GRAND CENTRAL**

13.9

**ROUTE FROM
GRAND CENTRAL**

Take the Metro North
Railroad, Harlem Line
(Harlem Outbound)
and get off at Woodlawn.

NEAR THE BREATHTAKING BEAUTY OF VAN CORTLANDT PARK, in the northernmost point of the Bronx, lies the community of Woodlawn. Half of Woodlawn is in the Bronx, but the other half is technically in the city of Yonkers. It's bound by New York City, Westchester County, and Van Cortlandt Park. But no matter which side you're on, it feels 100 percent Irish. Welcome to the Emerald Isle, right here in New York City.

The area, originally called Woodlawn Heights, was primarily farmland in the early 1800s. However, in 1832, construction of the Harlem Railroad brought development to this small community. Further development continued with the construction of Woodlawn Cemetery in 1863. With the establishment of these expansive memorial grounds—where notables like Irving Berlin, Herman Melville, and Duke Ellington now rest—related businesses emerged: stone cutters for headstones, florist shops, housing for laborers and restaurants, and hotels for the bereaved.

Businesses related to the burgeoning growth of New York City began to develop in the 1890s. Irish laborers were hired to build the Croton Reservoir and Van Cortlandt Park's aqueduct to deliver 90 million gallons of water to New York City every day. They settled here building families, homes, and Irish institutions.

Unlike so many other neighborhoods today, Woodlawn has stayed the same over the past 100 years, mostly because its Irish roots run deep. Today the Irish are 6,000 strong in Woodlawn. Some are young, new Irish immigrants and others have families who have been here for three or four generations. In fact, it's not unusual for homes to be passed

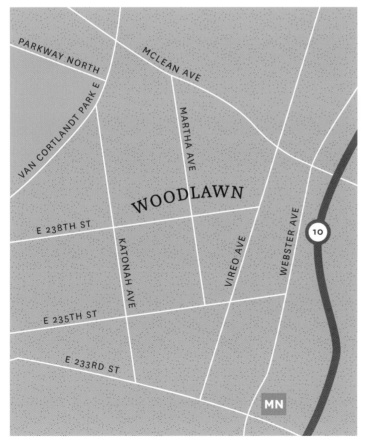

**MN** = Metro North stop
**Metro North** train stop, Woodlawn Station

# LITTLE IRELAND
## NEIGHBORHOOD GUIDE

### LITTLE IRELAND'S LOCAL FLAVORS

*Come for a typical Irish fry-up:*
**Fried eggs, a rasher of bacon, blood sausage, black and white pudding, scones, and brown bread or Irish soda bread**

*Or try:*
**Corned Beef and Cabbage**

**Shepherd's Pie**

**Irish Sausage, Mash, and Baked Beans**

**Irish Stew**

## EAT

**Eileen's Country Kitchen**
964 McLean Avenue

**The Irish Coffee Shop**
946 McLean Avenue

**The Rambling House**
4292 Katonah Avenue

## NIGHTLIFE/BARS

**Rory Dolan's**
890 McLean Avenue

**Rockin Robins**
942 McLean Avenue

**Ned Devine's Saloon**
940 McLean Avenue

## SHOP

**Annie's Attic**
*Irish Gift and Craft Shop*
952 McLean Avenue

**Traditional Irish Bakery**
4268 Katonah Avenue

**The Butcher's Fancy**
961 McLean Avenue

**Prime Cut Butchers**
4338 Katonah Avenue

## VISIT

**St. Barnabas Church**
*(Local parish)*

**Van Cortlandt Park, Museum, and Golf Course**

BREAKFAST
DAILY 11AM – 3PM

IRISH BREAKFAST
ULSTER FRY          HOMEMADE
PANCAKES            BREAD &
FRENCH TOAST       SCONES
OATMEAL            DAILY
OMELETTES
SANDWICHES........and more.

SPECIAL
TO GO  MON–FRIDAY 6–11AM
EGG SANDWICH & COFFEE
2·50
WITH BACON 3·50

down from generation to generation. The streets are lined with neat and tidy brick and wood-framed houses nestled next to one another. The residents are proud of their homes and their neighborhood and have great civic pride. St. Barnabas Church is the spiritual home of Woodlawn as is the Oneida Triangle. Curiously, not many churches commemorate the Irish contribution of men who served in World War I. Woodlawn has a small town flavor, not surprising given most of its residents have their roots in the Land of a Thousand Welcomes. Katonah Avenue, running north-south, and McLean Avenue, running east-west, are the heart of Woodlawn, so don't be surprised to see a shamrock in the window of every Irish pub, bakery, restaurant, and gift shop. The stores have just as much of an Irish brogue as the locals.

This area is a great change of pace from the rest of the Manhattan and the Bronx—it's more laid back and relaxed. The residents here couldn't be more helpful. Ask them where to eat or drink, and they'll happily send you to their favorite pub or restaurant.

If you're here in the morning, have an Irish "fry" breakfast of fried eggs, white and black pudding, fried mushrooms, grilled tomatoes, potatoes, and scones. Or, later in the day have a meal of Shepherd's Pie, bangers and mash. When the sun goes down, the pubs light up, especially on Sundays. Locals watch Irish football and listen to live Irish music.

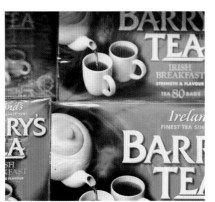

While you're coming to Woodlawn, think about bringing your golf clubs, and visit sprawling Van Cortlandt Park. Located on a verdant 1,000 acres, the park boasts the first public golf course in the United States as well as ballparks, soccer fields, and running trails. But when you're done with a day of sports, return to town and kick back, grab a Guinness, and enjoy this wee piece of Ireland. 🏌

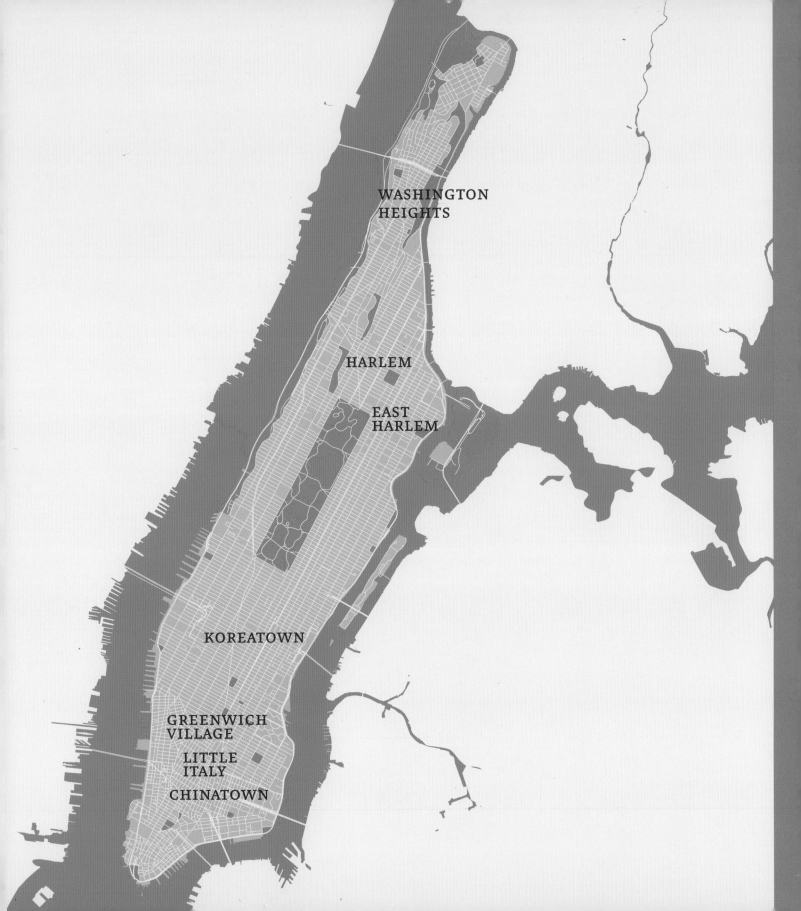

WASHINGTON
HEIGHTS

HARLEM

EAST
HARLEM

KOREATOWN

GREENWICH
VILLAGE

LITTLE
ITALY

CHINATOWN

# MANHATTAN

# EAST HARLEM'S "Little Mexico"

MILES FROM
GRAND CENTRAL

4.7

ROUTE FROM
GRAND CENTRAL

Take the 6 Subway
(Uptown) and get off
at 116th Street Station.

TRAVEL NORTH PAST THE GRAND LIMESTONE and brick façades of upper Park Avenue and you enter a whole other world. This community, unlike its closest neighbors, may not be rich in the conventional sense but it is rich none the less. To the residents of East Harlem, the neighborhood of "El Barrio" is an area steeped in Latino history with a strong cultural identity. Not so long ago this section of northeast Manhattan was primarily Puerto Rican, but today it has a growing Mexican population that is centered around East 116th Street and is known as "Little Mexico."

Like so many other neighborhoods this area has transitioned from one ethnic group to another. At various times, depending on the decade, this area has been called Jewish Harlem, Italian Harlem, and Spanish Harlem. Today, after all these name changes, it is called East Harlem.

But first came the farmers in the 17th century. It was the verdant land that brought the Dutch, French, Huguenots, Germans, Danes, and Swedes to settle here in the northern reaches of Manhattan. By the early 1800s the area became a mixture of Irish, Germans, and African Americans. Toward the end of the 19th century, the farmland had all but disappeared, and East Harlem's residents were poor Italian and Jewish immigrants living in low-slung, coldwater tenements. In fact, by the 1920s this neighborhood had the third largest Jewish population in the world. But as the population settled in and became more prosperous, they moved to the Bronx, Queens, and Brooklyn. The Italian population stayed on, for a time, and opened stores and community centers, and built more than

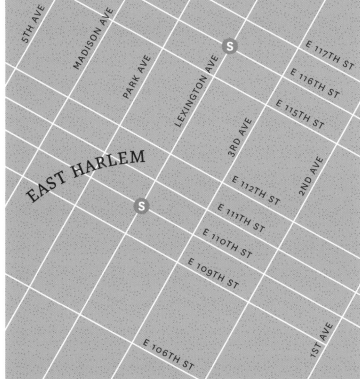

**S** = subway stop
**6** subway stop, 115th Street Station
**6** subway stop, 110th Street Station

# LITTLE MEXICO
## NEIGHBORHOOD GUIDE

### EAT

**Amor Cubano**
2018 Third Avenue at 111th Street

**Café Ollin**
*(Mexican)*
339 East 108th Street

**Camardas el Barrio**
*(Puerto Rican)*
2241 First Avenue at 115th Street

**Cuchifritos**
*(Puerto Rican fritters)*
168 East 116th Street

**El Barrio Juice Bar**
*(Shakes and natural juices)*
308 East 116th Street

**El Caribeno**
*(Latin American)*
1675 Lexington at 105th Street

**El Paso**
*(Mexican)*
1642 Lexington Avenue at 105th Street

**La Casa de Los Tacos**
*(Mexican)*
2277 First Avenue between 117th and 118th Streets

**Las Panteras Negras**
*(Mexican)*
2130 Second Avenue between 109th and 110th Street

### SNACKS

**La Tropezienne Bakery**
2131 First Avenue at 110th Street

**Savoy Bakery**
170 East 110th Street

**Valencia Bakery**
162 East 104th Street

**Samba Bakery**
165 East 106th Street

**Don Paco Lopez Panaderia**
2129 Third Avenue between 116th and 117th Streets

**La Lomita del Barrio**
*(Mexican sweets & produce)*
209 East 116th Street

**Mexico Lindo Grocery**
*(Mexican music, videos, sweets, and food)*
2265 Second Avenue between 116th and 117th Streets

### SHOP

**La Casa Blanca**
*(Meat market)*
127 East 110th Street

**Mi Pueblo Mini Mart**
*(Herbs, spices, and Mexican canned goods)*
224 East 116th Street

**Renaissance Cigar Emporium**
1825 Madison Avenue between 118th and 119th Streets

**Justo Botanica**
*(Herbal remedies and religious artifacts)*
134 East 104th Street

**Casa Latino**
*(For salsa music lovers)*
151 East 116th Street

### VISIT

**Julio de Burgos Cultural Center/Taller Boricua Gallery**
1680 Lexington Avenue between 105th and 106th Streets

**El Museo del Barrio**
*(Latin American Art)*
1230 Fifth Avenue

**Gallery for James de la Vega**
1651 Lexington Avenue between 104th and 105th Streets

**Restored Old Spanish Harlem**
104th Street between Lexington and Third Avenue

*While you're here, visit:*
**Graffiti Hall of Fame**
106th Street and Park Avenue

**The Modesto Flores Garden**
*(Poetry and community meetings)*
Lexington Avenue at 104th Street

**Mexican Futbol at Olmeca**
322 East 116th Street

**St. Cecilia's Church**
125 East 105th Street

---

### LITTLE MEXICO'S LOCAL FLAVORS

**Huevos Rancheros**
Eggs on a bed of tortillas topped with salsa, cheese, and black beans

**Burritos**
Meat, sausage, vegetables, and cheese wrapped in a tortilla

**Chili Rellanos**
Roasted Poblano peppers stuffed with cheese and deep fried

**Carne al Pastor**
Marinated roasted pork with onions and pineapple

**Arrachera Asada**
Marinated grilled skirt steak

**Chimichangas**
Deep-fried tortilla filled with cheese and chicken or beef and topped with melted cheese and salsa

20 churches like the majestic St. Paul's Roman Catholic Church and Our Lady of Mount Carmel Church.

Over time, however, Italian accents gave way to Spanish as Puerto Ricans began to move into the neighborhood. Suddenly East Harlem had morphed into Spanish Harlem. Today there is still a large Puerto Rican population. However, the wide, broad boulevard once known as Doctors' Row, a former middle class enclave in the midst of a one time impoverished East Harlem, is now the heart of "Little Mexico."

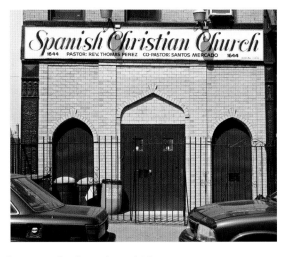

On almost any corner you'll find the rhythms of Hispanic daily life. The sounds of mariachi, rock en espagnol, and hip hop pour out of music stores. Clothing stores display Mexican flags, and at noon street vendors hawk tacos, tamales, sweets and gigantic corn tortillas made to order with your choice of meat fillings, salsa, avocado and shredded cheese. The numerous restaurants also offer countless Mexican dishes. In the bodegas or at the markets you'll find chocolates, salsa, mole, Mexican beer, and mountains of dried chilies. Not far from here kids play soccer and stickball on asphalt courts or shoot hoops in their futbol jerseys. A bit farther down on 106th Street and Park Avenue you'll run into a wildly painted wall so full of life that it is known across the world as "The Graffiti Hall of Fame."

There's plenty to see and eat and do here. But if you just stand still long enough, you'll probably see new immigrants who will no doubt add their own special flavor to the mix in this old neighborhood. ◇

# GREENWICH VILLAGE'S **"Little Britain"**

MILES FROM
GRAND CENTRAL

2.4

ROUTE FROM GRAND
CENTRAL

Take the 7 Subway (Westbound)
to 42nd Street/Times Square.
Transfer to the A Subway
(Downtown) and get off at
14th Street/8th Avenue.

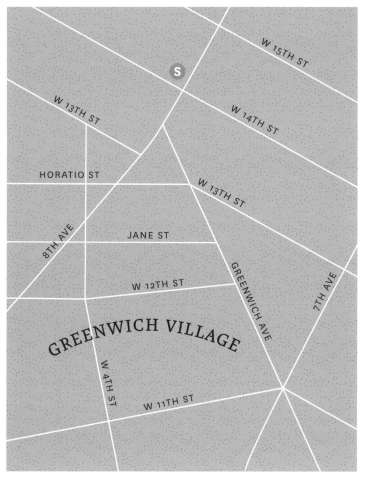

WHOEVER WOULD HAVE THOUGHT THERE'D BE another British invasion? But here in New York City's West Village is the littlest of "little" neighborhoods—Little Britain. There may not be a village green here, but there is Jackson Square, a delightful garden that is just a stone's throw from Greenwich Avenue, a tiny oasis devoted to all things British. So, though it might be a stretch to call this a British neighborhood it is where British ex-pats go for a taste of the U.K.

Unlike other communities that are steeped in history, this section of Manhattan has a relatively brief story to tell. True enough, these streets were once Indian trails, which were then settled by the Dutch and later occupied by the British. But by 1783, Americans had thrown the British out, and since then it has been inhabited by former colonists and the New Yorkers who have settled here for generations.

But the British are back and in the last 15 years they've opened charming tea shops, restaurants, and markets specializing in their national fare. It's not rare to find British models, actors, or other ex-pats—even those in financial services—craving English comfort food to satisfy their longing for a taste of home.

If you go to one of the local tea shops, you'll find Welsh rarebit, bangers and mash, and of course, tea sandwiches. Or head off to one of the local pubs where you can find everything from fish and chips to fried Mars bars. For those who want to fill their cupboard with British goodies, the British market on

**S** = subway stop
**A, C, E, L** train stop, 14th Street Station

# LITTLE BRITAIN
## NEIGHBORHOOD GUIDE

### LITTLE BRITAIN'S LOCAL FLAVORS

**Batter Fried Fish and Chips**
with mushy peas

**Bangers and Mash**
with battered sausage

**Steak and Kidney Pie**

**Welsh Rarebit**

**Shepherd's Pie**

**Roast Beef and Yorkshire Pudding**

**Tea Sandwiches**

**Fried Mars Bars/Toffee Crisp**

## EAT

**A Salt & Battery**
112 Greenwich Avenue between Jane and Horatio Streets

**Tea & Sympathy**
108 Greenwich Avenue between Jane and Horatio Streets

## SHOP

**Carry on Tea and Sympathy**
(British sweets)
110 Greenwich Avenue

**Myers of Keswick**
(British delicacies)
634 Hudson Street between Horatio and Jane Streets

*It may not be "Little Britain," but while you're on Greenwich Avenue check out these great places as well:*

## EAT

**Gusto Restaurant**
(Italian)
60 Greenwich Avenue

**41 Greenwich Restaurant**
(American)
41 Greenwich Avenue

**Wogie's Bar & Grill**
(Philly steaks and beer, sports bar)
39 Greenwich Avenue

## SHOP

**Mxyplyzyk**
(Housewares)
125 Greenwich Avenue

**Flight 001**
(Travel gear)
96 Greenwich Avenue

**Alphabets**
(Inexpensive, quirky gifts)
47 Greenwich Avenue

Hudson Street offers old English culinary favorites. Here you can buy authentic Shepherd's Pie, pork pie, scones, jams, chutneys, or British sweets like Cadbury Flakes or Curly Wurlys.

There's a tongue-in-cheek feeling to all of this. The shops are packed with tea towels with pictures of the Queen, Union Jacks, and all sorts of funky British memorabilia. The locals, ex-pats, and tourists have all come to experience these quirky, charming little streets with the unmistakable vibe of Mother England.

After all, this area is one of New York's oldest neighborhoods, surrounded by beautiful, low-slung brownstones. So if you find yourself exploring this part of downtown, stop in for a spot of tea and take a respite from the frenetic energy that is New York City. ⌣

# HARLEM'S "Little Senegal"

MILES FROM
GRAND CENTRAL

5.8

ROUTE FROM
GRAND CENTRAL

Take the 7 Subway
(Westbound) to 5th Avenue
Station. Transfer to the
B Subway (Uptown) and get
off at 116th Street Station.

AT FIRST GLANCE, THIS AREA LOOKS JUST LIKE any other part of Harlem, but soon enough, it becomes a blur of people dressed in vivid multi-colored hues. The women are resplendent in bright turbans, long, beautifully refined embroidered dresses, and armloads of jangly bracelets. In dark robes, the men appear somewhat more subdued and stride down the street exhibiting their own unique sort of elegance. Here is "Little Senegal"—a piece of West Africa right here in a three-block area around 116th street and Frederick Douglass Boulevard in Harlem.

Immigrants from Senegal and other West African nations began arriving in Harlem in the mid-1980s when their homeland suffered from a severe drought and poor economy. They, like all immigrants to this country, came with hopes of a better life and found one of New York City's most historic neighborhoods a fine place to put down roots. Today Little Senegal is as distinctive within Harlem as is Harlem within New York City.

But just as you can't take Harlem out of New York City, you can't take Little Senegal out of Harlem. Harlem is a reflection of New York City's growth, a microcosm of its continuing evolution. In its 400-year history, Harlem has been home to the Dutch, English, Irish, Eastern European Jews, Italians, African Americans, and now an enclave of West African immigrants. Harlem has been lush farmland, a wealthy suburb, and a victim of urban decay. Today, Harlem is in the midst of another renaissance and

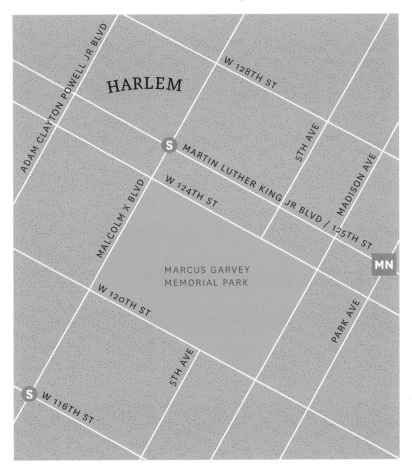

S = subway stop   MN = Metro North stop
2, 3 subway stop, 125th Street Station
2, 3 subway stop, 116th Street Station
**Metro North** train stop, Harlem-125th Street Station

# LITTLE SENEGAL
## NEIGHBORHOOD GUIDE

### EAT

✓ **Africa Kine**
*(African)*
256 West 116th Street

**Sokhna**
*(African/Moroccan)*
225 West 116th Street

✓ **Dibiterie Cheikh**
*(Senegalese)*
231 West 116th Street

**Le Baobab**
*(Senegalese)*
120 West 116th Street

**Africa Restaurant**
247 West 116th Street

✓ **Zoma**
*(Ethiopian)*
2084 Frederick Douglass
Boulevard at 113th Street

### SHOP

✓ **Malcolm Shabazz
Market**
116th between Lenox and
Fifth Avenues
*100 stalls selling African
jewelry, art, drums, masks,
cloth, and more*

**N. Harlem Clothing Store**
114 West 116th Street
*Moved*

### VISIT

**Malcolm Shabazz
Mosque**

*While you're here, visit the
rest of Harlem...*

### EAT

**Amy Ruth's**
*(Southern food)*
113 West 116th Street

**Dinosaur Bar-B-Que**
646 West 131st Street

**Sylvia's**
*(Soul food)*
328 Malcolm X Boulevard

### VISIT

**The Studio Museum
in Harlem**
*Works of contemporary
black artists*
144 West 125th Street

**Abyssinian Baptist
Church**
132 Odell Place at 138th
Street

**Canaan Baptist Church**
132 West 116th Street

**Mt. Morris Historic
District**
*(Restored 19th-century
townhouses)*
Lenox Avenue between
120th and 124th Streets

**St. Nicholas Historic
District**
*(Strivers Row land-marked
architectural gems)*
Adam Clayton Powell
Boulevard between 138th
and 139th Streets

### NIGHTLIFE/BARS

**The Apollo Theater**
*(Music, amateur night)*
253 West 125th Street

**Lenox Lounge**
*(Dinner and jazz)*
288 Lenox Avenue at 125th
Street

**Big Apple Jazz & EZ's
Woodshed Café**
*(Jazz performed 2 p.m. daily)*
2236 Adam Clayton Powell
Boulevard

---

**LITTLE SENEGAL'S
LOCAL FLAVORS**

**Thiebu Djen**
Traditional fish stew

**Lamb Mafe**
Lamb stew in peanut sauce

**Foufou**
Lamb and fish with okra
and plantains

**Pintade**
Grilled guinea fowl

**Thiakry**
Couscous, vanilla,
sour cream, and fruit